GW00645511

COMMENDATIONS
FOR

# *Equal to Rule*

As I read this book I could hear Trevor's voice; and in hearing his voice I could detect many things about him – his clear mind, warm heart and quick wit. But most of all, throughout this book, readers will have a sense of Trevor's love for the Lord, his Church, for men and women.

Every Church member, Presbyterian or not, will find in *Equal to Rule* a debate which will take them into the history of the Christian Church, the relevant passages of scripture and leave them in their present church setting. *Equal to Rule* is accessible to every thoughtful Christian. It will enlighten the mind and warm the heart.

It is my honour to commend *Equal to Rule* and I trust that many will benefit from reading it.

✢ *Rob Craig, Moderator of the General Assembly,*
*2013–14*

This book is essential reading for all who are concerned to know more and understand better the issues of gender equality within the Church – especially as they relate to leadership. Based on clear, biblical scholarship and demonstrating wise and thoughtful judgement, this piece of work is able to communicate with all those wrestling with this subject. It would be especially useful for Kirk sessions and congregations exploring the subject of those qualified for eldership within our own denomination. It should do much to help its readers to find their way through the maze of current beliefs about women in ministry and leadership and come to a prayerful biblically based understanding and experience. I thoroughly recommend Trevor's work to the whole Church at this time.

✣ *Mairisíne Stanfield, Minister of First Bangor*

Compelling, accessible and scholarly; *Equal to Rule* is a hymn to the breathtaking diversity, yet unifying complementarity of gender roles within ministry. This book illuminates, clarifies and faithfully outlines the biblical basis for the role of men and women in ministry. This is an important study and helpful companion for anyone journeying through the Presbyterian ministry in Ireland.

✣ *Rev. Karen Campbell, Kilbride Presbyterian Church*

A winsome, gracious and compelling explanation of the biblical and theological reasons why women and men are to share leadership as equals within the Christian Church. Trevor Morrow is a gifted communicator with a wonderfully easy-to-read style, but behind the scenes lies a great deal of thought and careful research. He writes out of a deep pastoral concern that women be encouraged and released to use their God-given gifts in the Church alongside men. Such joint leadership is God's design and strengthens the life and witness of the Church. *Equal to Rule* represents another significant evangelical voice supportive of women in leadership. While focused on the Presbyterian Church in Ireland, it is an excellent resource and I pray it will be read and used widely.

*✝ Dr Patrick Mitchel, Lecturer in Theology,
Irish Bible Institute, Dublin and ruling elder,
Maynooth Community Church*

EQUAL TO RULE

*Dedicated to*
*David, Doris, Ruth, Joseph, Keith, Dorothy,*
*Ian, Les, Trish, Janet, Frank, Brian, Carys,*
*Alan and Bernie – elders who have served with*
*me in Lucan Presbyterian Church.*

Trevor Morrow

# Equal to Rule

*Leading the Jesus Way*

*Why men and women are equal to serve in
leadership in the Christian Church*

the columba press

First published in 2014 by
**the columba press**
55A Spruce Avenue, Stillorgan Industrial Park,
Blackrock, Co. Dublin

Cover image: *Fractio Panis*, courtesy of the Photo
Pontifical Commission for Sacred Archaeology.
Illustrations: Kim Shaw

Layout by The Columba Press
Cover design by sin é design
Printed and bound by CPI Group (UK) Ltd, Croydon, CR0 4YY

ISBN 978 1 78218 149 1

# Contents

# Acknowledgments

It was while on sabbatical that I began to reflect on this subject. Mary Ann Richardson, a good and longstanding friend from Florida, offered me a condominium in Daytona Beach to study and write. In her inimitable way she provoked and challenged and encouraged me. I am indebted to her. Thanks too to those who saw my initial draft and made insightful and grammatical corrections; I am thinking of Victoria Carroll, John Dunlop, Ken Newell, Lorraine Kennedy Ritchie, Tony Davidson, Frank Sellar, Florence Craven, and Kevin Hargaden. The illustrations have helped to focus the primary emphases of each section. I am so glad I found Kim Shaw from Kilkenny Presbyterian Church to do these for me. She has done a first-rate job. Thank you to those who have written words of commendation; Patrick Mitchell from the Irish Bible Institute and an elder from Lucan, who helped plant the church in Maynooth, Mairisine Stanfield and Karen Campbell, friends who are having effective ministries in the Presbyterian Church in Ireland and, as I write, the Moderator of the General Assembly, Rob Craig, who has been a wise and godly leader. Stephen Williams is an outstanding reformed theologian and at the same time winsome with a servants heart. We have been close friends for years. I am honoured that he should have written the foreward for me. And especially thank you to Carys, my amazing wife and elder of the church who has lived with this project for years and still loves me.

# *Foreword*

We come across two prominent attitudes when we encounter disagreements over women's ordination or women in Church leadership. On the one hand, a number of people assume that the plain teaching of scripture prohibits it. On the other hand, for a number of people, it simply feels right and they do not get to grips with biblical teaching. We find these attitudes in PCI (Presbyterian Church in Ireland), as we do everywhere else. Both parties end up in the same place: reluctant to study the biblical text freshly and objectively, with the willingness to go where it leads.

Dr Trevor Morrow has written this book in order to show why we, in PCI, ascribe to men and women full equality in leadership in the churches on the basis of the teaching of scripture. It is the fruit of years not only of biblical study and preaching, but of experience in applying the gospel to the lives of women and men in different cultural contexts. It is written with passion, as it should be, a passion born of a conviction about what the Bible teaches in this matter, expressed with restraint and care, but with that deep concern for the witness of the Church of Jesus Christ which has been the mark of a blessed and distinguished ministry over a number of years.

I hope that everyone who reads it will weigh carefully what is said in this book. No one has to agree with everything in it, but let us not use any disagreements that we may have as an excuse for dismissing the conclusion. And let us not use our agreement with the conclusion as an excuse for not studying the matter carefully for ourselves. Our confidence in Jesus Christ and his word should mean that we think and walk in freedom, ready for self-correction, ready for instruction. Let those of us who have opposed the ordination of women be prepared to think again; let those of us who have supported it be prepared to ask ourselves whether we really have a biblical basis for doing so.

We all need to struggle – certainly I do – to undeceive ourselves in this, as in so many other matters. I may think that the Bible clearly proclaims that leadership in the churches should be male, but into my thinking goes a mix of biblical interpretation and a love of power and desire to preserve a status quo which keeps men on top. I may think that the Bible clearly directs us to a leadership in the churches which is male and female, but into my thinking goes a mix of biblical interpretation and an uncritical assimilation of wider cultural habits of thought which distorts my reading of the text. The fallout of our attitudes is often hurt, demoralisation, cynicism, aggression – those things which tear the Church of Jesus Christ apart as surely as does any doctrinal error.

For many years, I have looked up to Trevor Morrow in deep gratitude for his life, leadership and ministry. So I am privileged by this invitation to write a brief foreword. I have also been privileged to be a part of PCI for over eighteen years and am encouraged and edified by the many within it, leaders and 'laity' (as we call them!), women and men whose single-minded devotion to Jesus Christ shows that they have internalised what the Apostle Paul said: 'To live for me is

Christ.' So let us think for him, as part of our living for him, and may this book mightily help us to do so and lead us to the precious gift of knowing what it is to be a man and a woman in Christ.

*Stephen Williams*
*Union Theological College, Belfast*
*February, 2014*

*Preamble*

My grandmother was a cook in a big house in Co. Tyrone. She was 'in service'. Granny Barnes was like 'Mrs Bridges' from the TV series *Upstairs, Downstairs*. As a boy I would have visited her on a Saturday afternoon so that my Aunt Jenny, who lived with her, could go and do the shopping. She made me soda farls on the griddle and served them warm with lashings of butter. We would talk about her life 'downstairs'. For Granny, everyone and everything had their place. There was a pecking order. This was especially true about gender roles. I remember being berated for carrying in washing (I thought I was helping because it was beginning to rain). No, No, that was women's work. It wasn't right. People might see and what would they think. Men wheeling prams was somehow emasculating, as was doing laundry. She spoke bluntly on such issues, reflecting the world with which she was familiar. It just wasn't decent and respectable.

Many churches today are like living in the big house. We function as if we were in *Downton Abbey*. Although we cannot bring ourselves to sing:

> The rich man in his castle,
> The poor man at his gate,
> He made them, high or lowly,
> And ordered their estate.

Nevertheless, when it comes to gender, it's a world where men rule and women know their place. For some this is not just decent but it's God's design. It's how it's meant to be.

I have ministered in Lucan near Dublin for thirty years. The church is not just multi-national but representative of various church traditions and practices. This has raised all sorts of practical and pastoral issues of how we 'do' church. In new membership classes and in home visits I have been often asked why women and men share mutually in the leadership of Lucan Presbyterian Church. We have an almost equal number of men and women as elders and both genders are represented in those who have gone from us into the ministry of word and sacrament.

Sometimes these queries would come from those whose background is culturally patriarchal. At times, the questions would be from those whose church traditions forbade women from certain ministries for sacramental reasons. This would be true of those who had been raised Roman Catholic. There would also be those who have come from certain 'evangelical churches' where they had been taught that according to the Bible there were certain things a woman could and should not do. To have a role in the Church where they might be seen to be leading or teaching men was definitely not permitted. So how come LPC allowed this?

This book expresses how I have responded to such queries. This is not written to persuade those who hold a different view. It is not polemical. I am hoping that it will be of help to the wider Church as a practical resource when it comes to the electing of elders and the calling of ministers. It is meant to be a clear and succinct explanation of why on such occasions, according to the Code (The Book of the Constitution and Government of the Presbyterian Church in Ireland, par. 31) 'women shall be eligible for election on the same conditions as men'. Other Christian communities should also find it helpful in giving biblical reasons when they too practise gender equality and mutuality in leadership.

I am particularly concerned that women will experience in reading this the love and acceptance which Jesus brings in restoring them to be co-rulers with men over the new creation.

*Jesus made women feel very special*
*He affirmed them.* Think of that woman who had been bleeding for years and whose self-worth had been crushed, who in desperation touches him in a last-ditch effort to be healed. She had hoped her action would not be noticed because she was socially and ceremonially unclean. She is not only cured but Jesus commends her and it immediately transforms her self-image.

*He forgave them.* When he was confronted with a woman who was to be executed for adultery, Jesus felt compassion for her, forgave her and set her free without guilt.

*He taught them.* He encouraged Mary to join the men at a seminar in her home and also instructed her sister, Martha, so that she was able to give a better confession of who Jesus was than even Simon Peter.

*He honoured them.* He made them teachers of the Church: Mary his mother, whose insights and understanding are recorded in the gospels, and his selection of women to be the first witnesses to his resurrection.

*He made them part of his community.* Men and women were both disciples who travelled with him and women specifically helped to finance his Kingdom project.

No wonder they adored him, as is evident in a woman pouring expensive perfume on his feet, much to the outrage of a man who could only think about how much it was costing.

Dorothy Sayers, the English novelist and academic captures the mood of women regarding Jesus: They were

> first at the Cradle and the last at the
> Cross. They had never known a man like
> Jesus – there never has been such
> another. A prophet and teacher who
> never nagged at them, never flattered or
> coaxed or patronized; who never made
> arch jokes about them, never treated
> them either as 'The women, God help
> us!' or 'The ladies, God bless them!'; who
> rebuked without demeaning and praised
> without condescension; who took their
> questions and arguments seriously; who
> never mapped out their sphere for them,

never urged them to be feminine or
jeered at them for being female; who had
no axe to grind and no uneasy male
dignity to defend.

In Christ's Church today many women do
not feel special. They smile passively or
grimace as they once again have to listen to
male 'put down' humour. In spite of their
extraordinary gifts, which are being used in
almost every other area of life, in the Church,
they are asked to do 'women's things', like
make the tea, do the flower arrangements
and teach children in Sunday school. Even
when they are more spiritually mature, more
discerning and more godly than many men
and have proven themselves to be the
bedrock of the prayer life and mission
endeavours of the Church, they are
bypassed for leadership. On those occasions
when they have been chosen by a congregation to become an elder many will refuse
the invitation because they know what
people will say! So many women feel
devalued.

*It ought not to be this way*
It's good to be part of a community where,
in principle, women and men are 'equal to

serve' in the leadership. I write as a Presbyterian minister. It has been possible in the Presbyterian Church in Ireland for ruling elders to be women since 1926 and we have had women ministers from 1973.

We followed the example of other evangelical churches with a high view of scripture.

In the second century Ignatius wrote to the Smyrnaean Church, 'Salute Mary who was distinguished by her erudition and also the church which is in her home.' In his letter to the Antiochian fellowship, he reminded them to 'keep in remembrance Euodias [*a woman*], your deservedly beloved pastor'.

Our sister church the Waldensians in Italy, in the twelfth and thirteenth centuries, were excommunicated and driven to the mountains, not for heresy, but for having preachers, including women, who had not been sanctioned by the bishops.

Not surprisingly, the Quakers with their low view of recognised ministry, in the seventeenth century, made no difference between men and women leading. The Methodist Church has had women and men preaching and sharing leadership from the eighteenth century. They have just had their first women president in Ireland.

The Salvation Army has had men and women officers from its origins and currently their general is a woman. Significantly, the Pentecostalists and Charismatics, like the Assemblies of God or the Vineyard fellowships, and the Holiness churches, such as the Church of the Nazarene and the Free Methodists, from their beginnings, have ordained men and women to the ruling and teaching ministry.

The Church of Ireland has ordained women alongside men since 1990. In 2013 they ordained an overtly evangelical woman as their first female bishop.

Most of our members have never really thought much about what the Bible says around this subject. When it comes to the election of elders or the calling of a minister, some might say that since we have had male and female monarchs and presidents, and that there are men and women teachers, doctors, politicians, civil servants and trade unionists, whether an elder or a minister is a man or a woman is of little consequence. Traditionalists might struggle with the idea of women leaders. They would argue that they have always had male elders and ministers and they see no good reason for acting differently. The objections to women elders and ministers are often quite amusing, with some arguing that women themselves don't want it, that a woman would notice the state of the house when she visits, or that a man would feel intimidated by having to take directions from a woman (really)!

It is important for us to know the reasons why men and women can share as leaders in the ministry of our congregations. So, let me set out as clearly and concisely as I can why we as a church 'do as we do'. The arguments are all from the Bible because the Bible is our only reliable guide.

*Two things before we start*
First, there is nothing new in this. Scholars have written volumes on this subject. I have gleaned from, distilled and repackaged their research. I am particularly indebted to Kenneth Bailey. He is a theologian I have never met but his insights in this area cause the scriptures to make sense to me. So much of this book reflects his exegesis and perspective. At any rate what I have written is a popular version so that as many people as possible can have access to the key arguments.

Second, in order to keep the material focused I have not engaged with any alternative views. For those who want to pursue this, the resources section will be helpful.

## In the Beginning

We will begin at the beginning with the book of Genesis. It gives us three simple principles.

*Chapter 1 teaches us the equality of men and women*

> Then God said, 'Let us make mankind in our image, in our likeness, so that they may rule over the fish in the sea and the birds in the air, over the livestock and all the wild animals, and over all the creatures that move along the ground.'
>
> ☩ *Genesis 1:26*

> So God created man in his own image, in the image of God he created him; male and female he created them.
>
> ☩ *Genesis 1:27*

This tells us that men and women, individually, together, and equally reflect who

God is: 'in the image of God he created them; male and female he created them.' (Genesis 1:27)

And that individually, together and equally they are to rule over what he has made.

> God blessed them and said to them, 'Be fruitful and increase in number; fill the earth and subdue it. Rule over the fish in the sea and the birds in the air and over every living creature that moves on the ground.'
>
> ✣ *Genesis 1:28*

Adam could have said, 'Since I was made first, I'm in charge.' Or Eve could have said, 'I was made last and the climax of creation so I'm in charge.' There was none of that. From the outset men and women were called to give leadership as equals. This much is clear.

*Chapter 2 highlights that men and women are different and need each other*

The Lord God said, 'It is not good for the man to be alone. I will make a helper suitable for him.'

⚜ *Genesis 2:18*

Now the Lord God had formed out of the ground all the wild animals and all the birds in the air. He brought them to the man to see what he would name them; and whatever the man called each living creature, that was its name. So the man gave names to all the livestock, the birds in the sky and all the wild animals.

But for Adam no suitable helper was found. So the Lord God caused the man to fall into a deep sleep; and while he was sleeping, he took one of the man's ribs and closed up the place with flesh. Then the Lord God made a woman from the rib he had taken out of the man, and he brought her to the man.
The man said,

> 'This is now bone of my bones
> and flesh of my flesh;
> she shall be called "woman",
> for she was taken out of man.'

⚜ *Genesis 2:19–23*

Adam is described as being unfulfilled. It is not good that he is alone. He names the animals not because he wants to show who is boss, but because he is looking for a companion, but they do not meet his need. So, out of him woman is created and when he sees her, Adam gets so excited that be breaks into song (in fact the first poem in the Bible): 'bone of my bone, flesh of my flesh.' He recognises that she is the same as him but different. She has been made to be his 'helper'. Now this is a big word. It does not mean that she is there to run after him and to make sure he gets his slippers and cocoa at night. It's the word used for God as the one who helps us when we are in need. Woman is created to help man to realise his potential. Men, therefore, need women and women need men. This is true today whether we are married or single, are part of a nuclear family or live in community. Women and men complement each other.

*Chapter 3 is the sad account of mankind's moral rebellion against God and its dire consequences including male only rule*

To the woman he said,
'I will make your pains in childbearing
very severe;
with painful labour you will give birth to
children.
Your desire will be for your husband and
he will rule over you.'

✣ *Genesis 3:16*

To Adam he said, 'Because you listened
to your wife and ate fruit from the tree
about which I commanded you, "You
must not eat of it,"
'Cursed is the ground because of you;
Through painful toil you will eat food
from it all the days of your life.

✣ *Genesis 3:17*

It will produce thorns and thistles for you,
and you will eat the plants of the field.

✣ *Genesis 3:18*

By the sweat of your brow
you will eat your food
until you return to the ground,
since from it you were taken;
for dust you are
and to dust you will return.'

✣ *Genesis 3:19*

When this specific list is given of what it will be like in this broken world, you notice how women will desire after their husbands and he will rule over them. What women are desiring after here may be uncertain but what is clear is that men ruling over women, that is, being number one in a hierarchy of authority is the result of men and women having rebelled against God.

We have discovered that from the beginning women and men were equal in their calling to lead. However, equality did not mean they were the same. Men and women, being different, were to complement each other in their leadership. Men would lead as men. Women would lead as women. Individually and together it would show that they are godlike.

However, Genesis 3 tells us that the world is broken and needs to be fixed, which includes how men and women relate to each other and how we are to lead. So, in cultures around the world where men dominate 'the weaker sex', that is not how it ought to be.

The good news is that from the outset, God had a special plan to restore what he had made and make everything the way it was meant to be.

## Men and Women
## in the Old Testament

The rest of the Old Testament is not happy reading for most women. Stories, like Abram saying that his wife, Sarai, was his sister in order to save his own skin, even though he  knew that she would be taken into a harem, reflects what had been predicted through mankind's disobedience. As does the endless lengths women felt they needed to go through to provide children, and especially a son, for their husbands. Many of the laws were definitely male biased. If one could prove that your wife had slept with another man, both culprits were to be killed. However, your husband could sleep with a prostitute and it was not considered adultery. Women had to be virgins at marriage but not men. Polygamy was permitted for men but a woman could have only one husband. A man could divorce his wife but a woman could not divorce her husband. It was definitely a man's world.

Nevertheless, running parallel with this are glimpses of God's plan to make everything alright. We see this in three ways:

1. The Law of Moses, although not challenging male rule, sought to protect the woman from its excess. Here are some examples:

   + A woman accused of sexual promiscuity would have a court trial.

   + A man who raped a woman was held responsible.

   + There were regulations for the disposal of children, slaves and prisoners of war.

   + Punishments of men and women were to be proportionate to the crime.

   + Widows were to be cared for by their relations.

- ✧ Fathers could leave their inheritance to their daughters rather than to their sons.
- ✧ Children are commanded to honour both parents.
- ✧ Mothers and Fathers are instructed in the law and both teach their children.

Women, at that time, were certainly better off than they would have been living in one of the surrounding nations.

2. Throughout the Old Testament women are encouraged to fully participate in the life of faith. Here are some examples:
   - ✧ 'Women pray to the Lord for children and thereby influence the shape of sacred history as in the case of Rebecca, Rachel and Leah.' (*Bruce Waltke*)
   - ✧ Women and men were able to become Nazirites.
   - ✧ 'Women served at the Tabernacle, in spite of the fact that the Greek translators of the Septuagint

balked at the idea and rendered the phrase "women who fast".'
(*Walter C. Kaiser Jr*)

✢ Women attended and were welcome participants in all the festivals and celebrations.

3. However, two remarkable events in the Old Testament show the equality and complementarity of men and women in leadership being recovered. The list of prophets, priests and kings are almost exclusively male; nevertheless, there are striking exceptions.

The first is the ministry of Moses and his sister, Miriam. Moses is recognised as a prophet, an intercessor and leader of his people. Miriam too is given such a standing as a woman. She is identified as a prophetess, one who had received the word of God and was called to speak it into a particular situation. She led the people in worship with charismatic fervour, waving her tambourine and dancing in the celebrations of the Exodus. Sure she got it wrong when she criticised Moses's choice of a Cushite bride but the fact that God had spoken his word

through her previously was never
challenged. It's why her song is recorded
in the book of Exodus as part of God's
word. Here both a man and a woman,

Moses and Miriam, are called to speak
God's word as the prophets of God.

The second is during the time of the
Judges. You remember that these were the
years when 'everyone did what was right
in his own eyes'. The people of God were
in trouble and strong leaders were
needed to guide the people and to bring
victory over their enemies. A judge and a
commander were sent by God. The
military general was Barak and the judge

was a woman, Deborah. They were a team; Barak would not act without her presence. Deborah must have been quite a lady. She was a person of great intelligence and influence. She was also a prophet. As a judge she had to apply the law of God to specific cases. She was a ruling elder in the house of Israel. Here we see a woman being honoured as one who could not only speak the word of God (her words are recorded in scripture) but she was expected to give leadership in the oversight of God's people.

So, in the patriarchal Old Testament, we have women and men leading worship, speaking God's word and fulfilling the role of the ruling eldership.

*Jesus and the Difference He Makes*

God's plan to restore what had been lost at 'the fall' is realised in the coming of Jesus. How he established a fundamental change in the pattern of leadership for men and women in the community of faith is central to our understanding. His ministry began when the status of women in Jewish society was at a low point. The prayer offered three times a day by a Jewish male – 'Blessed art thou, our Lord and God, King of the Universe who hast not made me a heathen … a bondsman … or a woman' – says a lot. In the period between the writing of the Old and New Testaments, the perception of women among men deteriorated. This is seen in the writings of Ben Sirach, a Jewish aristocrat from the second century BC.

> Any iniquity is small compared to a woman's iniquity … From a woman sin had its beginning, and because of her we all die.
>
> ✢ *Sirach 25:19, 24*

> Better is the wickedness of a man than a
> woman who does good; it is woman who
> brings shame and disgrace.
>
> ✝ *Sirach 42:14*

All this makes Jesus' ministry quite extraordinary. He was the bridge between the old and the new. He was part of the Old Covenant and established the New Covenant.

He was a member of the old Israel with its practice of circumcision, the celebration of the Passover and worship in the temple at Jerusalem.

He had come to create a new Israel with the practice of baptism, the celebration of the Eucharist and worship where he is the temple, the priest and the sacrifice.

In terms of leadership, his choice of twelve was deliberate. They represented the twelve tribes of Israel. He was showing that he was doing a new thing, bringing into being a new Israel. To flag this up successfully and with continuity from the old, the identity of the Twelve was important: they had to be Jews not Gentiles; they had to be free not slaves; they had to be men and not women.

The new was to be different.

> ✝ Jesus strategically offered his
>   kingdom message to Gentiles of
>   all sorts.

- ✢ He spent time and offered hope, much to the outrage of the religious establishment, to the marginalised, social rejects and to slaves.
- ✢ He enthusiastically invited and encouraged women with men to be taught and trained for leadership.

The leaders of the new Israel could then be Jews or Gentiles, slaves or free, men or women.

Jesus' attitude to women and men in leadership is amazing.

1. At the time of Jesus, to teach a woman was considered almost blasphemous. A Rabbi from 2 BC wrote, 'Let the words of the Torah be burned rather than be

committed to a woman … If a man teaches his daughter the law, it is as though he taught her lechery.' (Sotah) Nevertheless, Jesus had both women and men as disciples. Some were even financing his ministry. Men and women were being trained together. (Luke 8:1–3)

2. He was willing to challenge the social norms to enable women to be taught. The incident at Mary and Martha's home illustrates this (Luke 10:38–42). Martha is distraught about Mary not just because she is neglecting her chores but because her behaviour seems weird. Mary is with the men in the wrong part of the house (the male-only quarters) and is 'seated at the feet of Jesus'. This is the phrase used for the process of being trained to become a Rabbi as when 'Saul sat at the feet of Gamaliel'. Martha believes that if this continues Mary will never find herself a husband and will end up a social outcast. Jesus on the other hand commends Mary for the choices she is making. He suggests it is great to have women being prepared for leadership.

3.  It was quite shocking that Jesus should have stopped to converse with a Samaritan woman with a dubious reputation, especially since the rules for Rabbis at that time stated that a Rabbi was never to speak with a woman in public, not even his own wife. She, no doubt, was amazed and flattered. But he then engaged in a theological discussion which was life changing for her. She subsequently, as a woman, became a teacher to her own people, an evangelist (John 4:1–42). This was a pattern in Jesus' ministry.

4.  When it came to the process of teaching the disciples, Jesus uses illustrations and parables which enable both genders to grasp its relevance for them. They are told side by side, showing that women and men were being trained at the same time. Examples of this are: the kingdom is like a mustard seed (which would be planted by men) or like yeast (which would be handled by women); in the parable of the lost sheep, it's about a man; the lost coin is about a woman; in the parable of the lost sons, the central figure (the father) is

a man but Jesus' description of him running demonstrates him behaving like a mother (a woman). This is such a major element of Jesus' ministry that Luke in writing his gospel uses (according to Ken Bailey, the New Testament scholar) twenty-seven such couplets or parallels, such as: the angel appears to Zechariah (a man) then to Mary (a woman); Jesus is brought to Simeon (a man) and then to Anna (a woman), and so on.

The point is that men and women are being discipled together to become leaders in the new mankind.

5. The high point of each of the gospels is the death and resurrection of Jesus. How men and women behave at this moment is important. The women disciples, perhaps because in a patriarchal but chivalrous society it is safe for them to be around someone being executed for insurrection, remain with Jesus to the end. The men, for fear of their lives, deny him, betray him or abandon him, with the exception of John. The women, over and against the men, are portrayed as being faithful. The resurrection accounts make the contrast bigger. It is women, who were not permitted to give evidence in a

court of law, who are the first to announce, through their encounter with angels and an empty tomb, that the Lord had been raised from the dead. The eleven men thought this was nonsense (Luke 24:1–11). Now here is what is significant: the basic qualification for an apostle was that they were witnesses to the Resurrection. Men subsequently came to believe but the first believing disciples were women.

The expectation of Jesus was that men and women would both become disciples. Circumcision was the Old Covenant sign of being part of the community of faith. It was exclusively for males. This meant a woman could be part of Israel only through her father, or husband, or a brother or son. Jesus replaced circumcision with baptism as the sign of being in the new Israel. It was offered to both women and men. Gender was no longer to be a source of division. Both men and women were to be taught as disciples together and to share as one in the fulfilment of the Great Commission.

In anticipation of what had been promised, both men and women waited together in prayer to see fulfilled the prophecy of Joel:

In the last days, God says, I will pour out
my Spirit on all people.
Your *sons and daughters will prophesy*,
your young men will see visions,
your old men will dream dreams.
Even on my servants, *both men and women*,
I will pour out my Spirit on those days,
and *they will prophesy*.

✢ Acts 2:17–18

It is not surprising, therefore, that in the
early Church, empowered by the Holy
Spirit, men and women are listed in
leadership.

## Men and Women
## in Leadership Together

If paradise was to be restored and men and women were to reflect their godlikeness by having authority together, then we would expect to see this in the new mankind which Jesus had created. In fact, in the early Church, this is what we discover.

1. There were *prophets*. Men like Judas and Silas (Acts 15:32) and Agabus (Acts 21:10), and women like the daughters of Philip the evangelist (Acts 21:9) and the

women who prophesied in the Corinthian Church. The Church was built on
the apostles and prophets so these men
and women held an important role in the
early Church.

2. There were *deacons/ministers*. Men like
Timothy (1 Timothy 4:6) and women like
Phoebe (Romans 16: 1–2). The same
word, *diakonos*, is used for both. They
were honoured by being given this office
by the Church. Of Phoebe, John Calvin
wrote: 'He begins by commending
Phoebe … first on account of her office,
because she exercised a very honourable
and holy ministry in the church.'

3. There were *Bible teachers and theologians*.
Women like Priscilla and men like Aquila
(Acts 18: 24–8). When Apollos, the
eloquent and able preacher from
Alexandria appears in Ephesus he is
commended for his knowledge but we
are told 'he only knew the baptism of
John', so this woman and man team
moved into action 'but when Priscilla and
Aquila heard him they took him and
expounded to him the way of God more
accurately'.

4. There were *apostles* (other than the Twelve), who had a unique status of authority and respect in the early Church. They were witnesses to the Resurrection and had received a specific commission from Christ. Men like James, Barnabas, and Andronicus. And women like Junia (Romans 16:7). For nearly fourteen hundred years this was understood by the Church to be a woman. However, a fellow called Aegidius de Columna found it so incredible that a woman could be an apostle that he changed the name to the masculine Junias. As almost every commentator recognises, there is no evidence of that name anywhere else. Even St Chrysostom, who was no feminist, said, 'Oh what a blessed woman Junia must have been to have been called an apostle.' The early Fathers, Arabic and Syriac Christianity, and the authorised version of the Bible all concur. The evidence is overwhelming. There was a woman apostle ministering alongside men.

5. In Romans 16 we have *Paul's women's hall of fame*. Here are listed Persis, Tryphena and Tryphosa, whom he describes as those 'who work hard in the Lord'. The

same phrase he uses in 1 Thessalonians 5:12, and 1 Timothy 5:17 to describe men who are in ministry and exercise authority in the Church. In Philippians 4:2–3, Euodia and Syntyche he describes as co-workers 'who have contended at my side in the cause of the gospel'. Again this implies equality in ministry in that he uses the same language to describe his relationship with Timothy.

Here we have in the life of the early Church 'radical community' life in which men and women together are rediscovering the joy and privilege of being part of this new creation in Christ.

Professor Tom Torrance from Edinburgh, in his booklet on the ministry of women refers to one of the earliest Catacomb paintings in Rome in the Capella Greca. It is from within a century after the death and resurrection of Christ. It is known as the *Catacomb of Priscilla* and appears as the cover image of this book. As you can see in what is known as the *Fractio Panis*, there are seven elders seated in a semicircle behind the communion table. Torrance contends there were seven because, according to the Jewish Mishnah, if a community were a hundred and twenty strong they were allowed to have seven elders presided over by an 'Archsynagogos'. They were to be arranged, according to the Mishnah, 'like the half of a round threshing floor so that all might see one another'. This painting, according to Torrance, gives us a vivid glimpse into the assembly of one of these small congregation of believers with their seven presbyters. Aquila and Priscilla, and five others. Priscilla is seated to the right of one who, presumably, is her husband. She is, says Torrance, actively engaged in the Eucharistic rite, concelebrating with men, the breaking of bread.

The Apostle Paul is the great champion of this cause. His banner statement is in Galatians:

> So in Christ Jesus you are all children of
> God through faith, for all of you who
> were baptised into Christ have clothed
> yourselves with Christ. There is neither
> Jew nor Gentile, neither slave nor free,
> nor is there male and female, for you are
> all one in Christ Jesus.
>
> ✣ *Galatians 3:26–8*

This captures his passion. He is not saying that now Jews and Gentiles, slaves and free, men and women are to be saved. This was never in question. No he is affirming that the old divisions have now been removed in the new society created by Christ. All are to have equal status and standing in the Church. As Professor N. T. Wright from St Andrews points out, when it comes to the gender issue, as a source of potential division, Paul is even stronger than many modern English translations would indicate. It ought to read: 'There is neither Jew nor Greek, slave nor free, no male and female.' He deliberately changes the conjunction. The notion of men and women being equal was obviously a bridge too far for some of the early believers.

## Some Pastoral Issues
## all this Creates for the Early Church

Putting this equality and complementarity into practice in the Jewish, Greek and Roman patriarchal society was not going to be easy. It was counter cultural. This is not how people thought or behaved. Jesus had initiated a new thing and it inevitably created major pastoral issues for the first generation of Christians.

The practice of Gentiles becoming part of this new faith community without them becoming Jews was a major source of tension. A special general assembly had to be called in Jerusalem to deal with the issue. Paul wrote his letter to the Galatians to combat those Jewish Christians who wanted to go back to the old ways.

The issue of slavery as a social phenomenon, which was challenged by the very existence of the Church, was addressed more pragmatically as in the letter to Philemon.

However, the seeds of its ultimate abolishment were planted.

It is not surprising, therefore, that the implications of women and men sharing together leadership as equals, without being equivalent, created major pastoral issues for the New Testament Church. Four in particular stand out.

We need to understand that each of these situations emerged out of the apostolic Church seeking to live out the implications of 'the new mankind' over and against the Jewish, Greek and Roman world. These were real issues for the early Church only because they were doing things differently from the prevailing culture.

To see how the Apostle Paul addresses each of them, we need to place ourselves in the world of the first century. There are major cultural factors at play. We ought not to read what was happening through the eyes of a twenty-first century western Christian but rather we need to immerse ourselves in the context of the apostolic Church. Some of them seem odd to us, like what we should wear on our heads or the importance of a woman wearing a veil. Presbyterians may not be too familiar with services in chaos, with strange languages not being interpreted, speakers interrupting each other and women chatting and asking questions all at the same time, but Paul has to deal with this. We may be used to women not being allowed to preach but we do not stop them going to the hairdressers or shopping for attractive clothes. The Apostle seems to insist on both. These passages are not easy to understand. Let's deal with them in turn.

PASTORAL ISSUE ONE

## *Marriage – The Jesus Way*

Whether you were a Jew, a Greek or a Roman, in marriage man was the boss. He was the father of the household. He made the decisions of significance. How could the pattern which Jesus established be practised in the Greek and Roman world? How could men and women be equal in their leadership of the family?

Aristotle expressed the common view. He argued that 'the man rules in accordance with his worth because he is superior'. 'For although there may be exceptions to the order of nature, the male is by nature fitter for command than a female.' Aristotle believed that the higher honour should go to the better. 'The friendship of man and wife,

again, is the same that is found in an
aristocracy; for it is in accordance with virtue
the better gets more of what is good.'

The Jesus way was different. The Apostle,
by contrast, sets it out in his classic statement
on Christian marriage:

> Submit to one another out of reverence
> for Christ.
>
> Wives, submit yourself to your
> husbands as to the Lord. For the husband
> is the head of the wife as Christ is the
> head of the church, his body, of which he
> is the Savior. Now as the church submits
> to Christ, so also wives should submit to
> their husbands in everything.
>
> Husbands, love your wives, just as
> Christ loved the church and gave himself
> up for her to make her holy, cleansing her
> by the washing with water through the
> word, and to present her to himself as a
> radiant church, without stain or wrinkle
> or any other blemish, but holy and
> blameless. In this same way, husbands
> ought to love their wives as their own
> bodies. He who loves his wife loves
> himself. After all, no one ever hated his
> own body, but he feeds and cares for it,
> just as Christ does the church – for we are
> members of his body. 'For this reason a
> man will leave his father and mother and
> be united to his wife, and the two will

become one flesh.' This is a profound
mystery – but I am talking about Christ
and the church. However, each one of
you also must love his wife as he loves
himself, and the wife must respect her
husband.

✠ *Ephesians 5: 21–33*

We have all been to marriage services
where the reading begins at verse 22. 'Wives,
submit yourself to your husbands' and the
congregation reckons the position of the
husband as the boss is being reinforced from
scripture. In fact the section begins with
verse 21, where husband and wife are being
asked to submit or to be subject to each
other. Marriage, for Paul, is between a man
and a woman who are equal. This is how it
was at creation before the fall and now has
been reestablished in Christ in the new
creation. So Paul is now dealing with the
practical implications for Christians practising marriage in a hierarchical society.

To submit does not mean to obey. That is
what children and slaves are to do
(Ephesians 6:1, 5). Instead, Paul deliberately
chooses a different word. Anyway, to obey
each other would be silly and unworkable.
'To submit' means something like 'to defer'

as we do at the general assembly or at presbytery when the moderator stands or chooses to speak. We give him (or her) their leadership role. In marriage we are to so submit to each other. In doing so we honour and recognise the giftedness and calling of each other to lead. This is how equality in Christian marriage is to be expressed. In fact when it comes to the bedroom, Paul becomes even more specific.

> The marriage bed must be a place of mutuality – the husband seeking to satisfy his wife, the wife seeking to satisfy her husband. Marriage is not a place to 'stand up for your rights.' Marriage is a decision to serve the other, whether in bed or out.
>
> ⚘ *The Message: 1 Corinthians 7:4*

Nevertheless, it is obvious that men and women are different. So Paul applies the principle of mutual submission first to the woman and then to the man.

'Wives, *submit* yourself to your husband's as to the Lord.' A woman, therefore, is to submit freely, without coercion or force as she does to the Lord himself, because the Lord has not brought her to faith with threats and intimidation but with love and compassion. She will not, therefore, submit to her husband with gritted teeth out of duty but with enthusiasm out of grace.

The reason for this, says Paul, is that 'the husband is the head of his wife as Christ is the head of the church'. Well, what does 'head' mean?

Obviously, the primary meaning is what is between our shoulder blades on our bodies – the cranium. It is being used here by Paul as a metaphor, a picture. But, what is Paul saying in using this picture? At this point scholars disagree.

He could mean by head 'preeminence', that is the one who is seen to be at the top – like the face of the family. Rather like an Irish president or a Presbyterian moderator who has been given a standing or status without any real authority.

Head could mean 'having authority over', as in a headmaster. This is its most common usage in the English language.

However, it could also mean 'the source' or 'origin' as in 'the head of a river'. It was F. F. Bruce, the leading evangelical New Testament scholar of the twentieth century, who first clearly showed this. The context of how Paul uses this word should help us.

How is Christ the head of the Church? Paul uses that expression on four other occasions in his letters. On each of these occasions he could mean 'preeminent'. However, as Gilbert Bilezikian, from Wheaton College and the primary theologian of the Willow Creek churches, points out, not once does it mean 'having authority over'.

Read the verses for yourself. You can see that in each case it is about empowering and resourcing the Church.

> And God placed all things under his feet and appointed him to be head over everything for the church, which is his body, the fullness of him who fills everything in every way.
>
> ✣ *Ephesians 1:22–3*

✣ Christ gives the Church fullness. He ensures its growth.

> Instead, speaking the truth in love, we will grow to become in every respect the mature body of him who is the head, that is, Christ.
>
> ✣ *Ephesians 4:15–16*

✣ Christ, as the head, provides the Church with growth.

> And he is the head of the body, the
> church; he is the beginning and the
> firstborn from among the dead, so that in
> everything he might have the supremacy.
>
> ✝ *Colossians 1:18*

✝ Christ is supreme over all and through
his resurrection, as the head gives life to
his Church.

> They have lost connection with the head,
> from whom the whole body, supported
> and held together by its ligaments and
> sinews, grows as God causes it to grow.
>
> ✝ *Colossians 2:19*

✝ Christ is the source of life for the Church.
It is he who causes it to grow.

These verses are, without exception, about
empowering or enabling the Church to
become. He causes the Church to grow, to
flourish, to become one.

Paul's argument is, therefore: Christ is our
life-giving source. We have been brought
into existence through him. He, therefore,
leads as a servant who enables us to become
what he has called us to be.

The husband as 'the head of his wife' is
then a reference to creation. He is 'the
source'. Woman was taken out of the side of

man to express her equality, but yet from him so that she might defer to him as her 'origin'. So a wife is to honour her husband. She will do all within her power to enable him to realise his potential. This will be no passive, 'Uriah Heep' type submission, but rather through challenging, encouraging, questioning and loving, a wife will take delight in her husband becoming what he was meant to be.

Now in the same way, the husband will express his submission in marriage by loving his wife as Christ loved the Church. He will be her servant. If necessary he will lay down his life for her. A husband, therefore, should make his wife feel overwhelmingly loved. He will sacrifice everything for her – his career, his hobbies, and his reputation. He will, like Jesus, become her servant and with a towel and basin wash her feet.

This is marriage, the new creation way. It's the Jesus way. It was radically in conflict with the Greek and Roman culture and it is with ours.

PASTORAL ISSUE TWO

## *Men and Women Leading Worship Together – The Jesus Way*

Again, we need to see that this is only a pastoral issue because men and women are behaving in leadership in a manner which is at odds with the norms of that time.

We get so used to how we do things that we assume that's the way it is meant to be. Our worship services, whether they are a psalm and hymn sandwich or a multi-visual event, they become our 'culture'. They are, 'the way we do things around here'. Change is not easy for any of us. For most ministers and elders, steering a congregation through 'how we are to worship' with Scottish metrical psalms, eighteenth-century hymns and contemporary spiritual songs is an ongoing challenge. Paul was confronted by a similar problem in Corinth.

Corinth was not an easy church. Paul lists the backgrounds of those who were members.

Or do you know that wrongdoers will
not inherit the kingdom of God? Do not
be deceived: neither the sexually
immoral nor idolaters nor adulterers nor
male prostitutes nor homosexual
offenders nor thieves nor the greedy nor
drunkards nor slanderers nor swindlers
will inherit the kingdom of God. And
that is what some of you were.

✟ *1 Corinthians 6:9*

There were a number of Jews present in the
new Christian community who were
familiar with the patterns in the synagogue.
For the Greeks this was all fresh and new. As
Christians, when they came together what
were they meant to do? How were they to
worship?

For both the Jews and the Greeks what was different in the Corinthian fellowship was that the men and women exercised ministries of leading in worship and in speaking prophetically. Paul saw this latter ministry as the most important in worship. It is as preaching the word of God is to us.

> But the one who prophesies speaks to people for their strengthening, encouragement and comfort.
>
> ✝ *1 Corinthians 14:3*

In the Jewish synagogue only men spoke and in Greek society women were so marginalised that they had to establish their own religions to practise any faith. Some Jews had written to Paul with a number of pastoral concerns. This is one of them. How were they to cope with women and men both taking part in the service of worship especially when it came to what you are wearing on your head? This may seem strange to us but for the Christians in Corinth this was a big deal. Remember this was a different culture to ours.

To understand their concerns, Kenneth Bailey (the New Testament scholar, who has spent his entire ministry looking at how they do things in the Middle East and applying it to understanding the Bible) tells us that we need to appreciate their psychology. In that culture people find their significance and identity not in what they do or even in their family but in their origin, where they have come from. Here was the issue for the believers in Corinth: when you show 'your glory', it reveals who you are and unveils your origin. It says where you have come from, your background, history and source. So, especially for the Jews, how one behaved in worship with regard to what you did or did not wear on your head was important. As you spoke your glory was revealed and, therefore, your source or origin.

> But I want you to realise that the head of every man is Christ, and the head of the woman is man, and the head of Christ is God. Every man who prays or prophesies with his head covered dishonors his head. But every woman who prays or prophesies with her head uncovered dishonors her head – it is just as though her head were shaved. For if a woman does not cover her head, she might as well have her hair cut off; but if it is a disgrace for a woman to have her hair cut off or her head shaved, then she should cover her head.
>
> A man ought not to cover his head, since he is the image and glory of God;

but the woman is the glory of man. For man did not come from woman, but woman from man; neither was man created for woman, but woman for man. It is for this reason that a woman ought to have authority over her own head, because of the angels.

Nevertheless, in the Lord woman is not independent of man, nor is man independent of woman. For as woman came from man, so also man is born of woman. But everything comes from God.

Judge for yourselves: is it proper for a woman to pray to God with her head uncovered? Does not the very nature of things teach you that if a man has long hair, it is a disgrace to him, but that if a woman has long hair, it is her glory? For long hair is given to her as a covering. If anyone wants to be contentious about this, we have no other practice – nor do the churches of God.

✝ *1 Corinthians 11:3–16*

Here we have a pastoral issue only because both women and men were publically exercising leadership in worship and speaking prophetically the word of God. The cultural difficulty was in how they were doing it. The issues concerned what they were or were not wearing and what this was communicating to those who were present.

Let me summarise what Paul is saying here as he deals with this: a man reveals his glory and displays his origin by having his head uncovered. It's as if he is acting like a mirror. As he ministers without a covering on his head people, therefore, will see his origin or source because 'the source [the head] of every man is Christ'.

Similarly, a woman, if her head is uncovered she too will reflect the glory of her origin. However, in her case the origin that is seen is not Christ. Because 'the source [the head] of every woman is man'. This will take away from the glory of God. So, therefore, a woman should cover her head.

All this, Paul reasons, is because:

1. *The head, the source or origin of every man is Christ.*

   Man, being created directly by God has, therefore, his origin in Christ.

2. *The head, the source or origin of every woman is man.*

   Woman was formed out of man who is, therefore, her origin.

3. *The head, the source or origin of Christ is God.*
   As the eternally begotten of the Father, Christ has his origin or source in God.

It is significant to see that the earliest interpretation of the metaphor of 'head' as source or origin in this passage is from Cyril of Alexandria in the fifth century. He argues:

> Thus we can say that 'the head of every man is Christ' for he was made by him …
> but the head of the woman is the man, because she was taken out of his flesh …
> likewise 'the head of Christ is God', because he is of him (*ex autou*) by nature.'
>
> ✝ *Ad Arcadiam et Marianam 5.6*

Here it is evident that in the Greek world, the idea of 'head' being a source of supply and a support for the body's systems was a natural metaphor. This became especially important in the early debates about Jesus because it avoided placing Christ 'under' God in a hierarchy or any form of subordination.

This is an odd passage. We do not have the same psychology or mindset that created these cultural issues for the Corinthian Church. The primary relevance of this for us today is that when men and women are ministering they are not to wear anything or do anything that will take away from the focus of their ministry or to distract from the glory of God. Should we then be wearing

Geneva gowns or academic hoods? On occasions they may add to our authority but they may also take from it. Similarly the wearing of Jon Snow ties or designer dresses could easily become a talking point without reference to what is being said or prayed? Image is important.

In fact, Paul now contends that when a woman is speaking in public worship what she is wearing is more significant than what a man is wearing when he speaks.

This is his reasoning: man did not come from woman but woman came from man. He further elaborates: man was not created *because of* a woman's need but woman was created *because of* the man's need. Her authority is in being able to meet his needs. Now since in that culture the sign of her authority was the wearing of a veil. She should, therefore, wear this veil or head covering as a sign of her authority when she publically speaks.

The whole point is that the focus should be on the women speaking God's word and that nothing should take away from her authority as she does so.

Paul then adds that whoever is ministering, whether men or women, we are all interdependent. He expects that both will be involved in public ministry during corporate worship. Both genders need each other.

What is important is this: this strange and culturally related issue of what was appropriate to wear only became a pastoral concern because men and women were both exercising their ministries publically in the Church. Paul was showing how to make it culturally possible for that time.

Today in our society we ought to do whatever is necessary to enable women and men to minister so that they will be enabled to speak with authority and to the glory of God.

Later on in his letter Paul turns to the matter of the disorderly way in which the Corinthians did worship.

> What then shall we say, brothers and sisters? When you come together, each of you has a hymn, or a word of instruction, a revelation, a tongue or an interpretation. Everything must be done so that the church may be built up. If anyone speaks in a tongue, two – or at the most three – should speak, one at a time, and someone must interpret. If there is no interpreter, the speaker should keep quiet in the church and speak to himself and God.

Two or three prophets should speak,
and the others should weigh carefully
what is said. And if a revelation comes to
someone who is sitting down, the first
speaker should stop. For you can all
prophesy in turn so that everyone may
be instructed and encouraged. The spirits
of prophets are subject to the control of
prophets. For God is not a God of
disorder but of peace – as in all the
congregations of the Lord's people.

Women should remain silent in the
churches. They are not allowed to speak,
but must be in submission, as the law
says. If they want to inquire about
something, they should ask their own
husbands at home; for it is disgraceful for
a woman to speak in the church.

*✣ 1 Corinthians 14: 26–36*

This doesn't appear to be very Presbyterian because it wasn't. It was closer to what
we might describe as a home group meeting.
Lots of people are taking part. This was a
new church with young converts and they
were learning, but the services were out of
control. Paul explains that such events are
meant to edify so people should understand
what is being said and done. He surmised
that if someone had been a visitor to the
church they would have reckoned it was a

mad house. Instead, says Paul, remember that the God we worship is not one of confusion but of peace. The service should, therefore, be decent and in order.

So, he tells them, when gifts and ministries are being exercised, in order that the worship will benefit those who are present, the three groups of people listed should be quiet.

The first are those who have spoken in an unknown language (in tongues) without an interpreter. One or two may exercise this gift, he says, but only if there is someone to interpret it.

The second are prophets (their gender is not indicated) who are to speak one at a time. But if someone else is ready to share, the first is to be silent so that the community will actually hear what is being said and so be edified.

The third group are women:

> Women should remain silent in the churches. They are not allowed to speak, but must be in submission, as the law says. If they want to inquire about something, they should ask their own husbands at home; for it is disgraceful for a woman to speak in the church.
>
> ☩ *1 Corinthians 14:34–5*

Clearly, women cannot lead in worship or exercise a prophetic ministry and be silent at the same time. Unless Paul is contradicting himself in a few paragraphs, this is not plausible. This cannot be a complete prohibition on women speaking in church.

This whole section is about orderly worship which will enable the listeners to understand and be edified. It is for this reason tongue speakers and prophets have been silenced. So then, what are these women up to which brings this censure?

In different cultures people behave in different ways in public worship. I minister in a multicultural congregation with people from every continent except the Antarctic. Our older members like services to be quiet and reverential. This is what they are used to. We have a crèche for babies and toddlers but mothers and fathers from parts of Africa are used to having their children with them possibly in buildings without roofs, where sound is not carried. All efforts to encourage some parents to take the children to crèche have so far been unsuccessful. One Sunday the sound of contributing children got so loud that I had to ask for a child to be taken out. The father was completely happy about this and beamed at me. It was a matter of cultural difference but for the rest of us to be edified it was necessary to do something!

Imagine what it was like in the Corinthian Church. The women would not have been formally educated. Their retention span was probably limited. They were at the service with their husbands but not necessarily sitting with them. They were chatting and asking questions. They did not think it odd. The volume of sound made it difficult for people to hear and, therefore, understand. So he tells these women to submit or defer to the leadership of their husbands and ask their questions at home. This endless chit-chat is no way to behave and is a disgrace.

Paul is, therefore, teaching the congregation in Corinth how to have decent and orderly worship in a new cultural setting. This, he believes, will lead to understanding and to the up building of the Church.

PASTORAL ISSUE THREE

## *How to Disciple Women –*
## *The Jesus Way*

1 Timothy 2:11–15 is the passage most frequently quoted as a sort of 'proof text' as to why women should be excluded from ministry as ruling or teaching elders.

> Therefore I want the men everywhere to pray, lifting up holy hands without anger or disputing. I also want the women to dress modestly, with decency and propriety, adorning themselves, not with elaborate hairstyles or gold or pearls or expensive clothes, but with good deeds,

appropriate for women who profess to worship.

A woman should learn in quietness and full submission. I do not permit a woman to teach or to assume authority over a man; she must be silent. For Adam was formed first, then Eve. And Adam was not the one deceived; it was the woman who was deceived and became a sinner. But women will be saved through childbearing – if they continue in faith, love and holiness with propriety.

☦ *1 Timothy 2:8–15*

Well what is the plain meaning of that passage?

☦ That men ought to raise their hands in prayerful worship.

☦ That women ought not to visit a hairdresser or be buying jewellery or attractive clothes.

☦ That women should know their place by being under a man's authority because women were responsible for the mess we are in and are easily deceived.

☦ That salvation is available to women by giving birth to children.

Is this really what Paul is saying or are we to respond, as some do, like Mary Slessor of Calabar, when she was confronted by such a restrictive passage, wrote in her Bible, 'Nay Paul laddie! This will na' do.'

To make sense of what Paul is saying it is helpful to know some things about what was happening in Ephesus. This was where Timothy, the recipient of this letter, was ministering.

⚜ As in Corinth, men and women are publically leading in worship.

The men, says Paul, are to do so in a manner without anger or without dispute but rather with their hands raised as one would in the public blessing of God's people. Paul is concerned that what they are doing outwardly is consistent with a godly attitude from the heart.

He then turns to the women in public ministry. Verse 9 begins, 'in the same way', or 'in like manner'. Now, he argues, when you are praying in public, dress in a way which is appropriate and not to draw attention to yourself. Instead by your actions and image you should be seen to be focusing on the worship of God.

☥ Women were involved in teaching and preaching because what they were teaching was the core of the problem.

The early stages of Gnosticism were present. This heresy taught that matter/the body was bad and only the spirit was good. In practice, fasting was then better than eating and celibacy was to be preferred to having sex and children. You can see this in 1 Timothy:

> The Spirit clearly says that in later times some will abandon the faith and follow deceiving spirits and things taught by demons. … They forbid people to marry and order them to abstain from certain foods, which God created to be received with thanksgiving by those who believe and who know the truth.
>
> ☥ *1 Timothy 4:1, 3*

☥ The city boasted of having one of the seven wonders of the world. It was a temple to Artemis (or Diana). It was a hundred foot longer than Croke Park. What is important to note is that it was run exclusively by women and somewhere they were able to exercise authority without restraint.

✢ Timothy was a good minister but a weak person. He was physically weak. (He was advised to take wine for his stomach problems.) He has become known as Timid Timothy because Paul when he writes has to encourage him not to be looked down on because of his age. (1 Timothy 4:12)

Put those together and it gives you a flavour of what was happening. Women from the temple had become part of the Church where they had begun to teach and practise a form of Gnosticism. They were strong and domineering women who were acting with an authority they had practised in the temple. Timothy and the men were being pushed around and browbeaten by them. When they gathered for worship, the men were angry and in dispute with the women. Even worse, heresy was being taught by these women in the Church.

Paul sets out a pastoral solution to the problem:

1. First and foremost these women are to be taught. Instead of having an argumentative spirit they are to learn in a quiet and undisturbed manner with deference or submission to those who know.

2.  These women should not be allowed to teach or to usurp their authority by having a domineering attitude toward men.

Paul could have chosen a word from normal usage, *proisteimi*, which means to direct or rule or manage. Instead he selects a stronger word, *authentein*, which means either to usurp authority or domineer. This is how it is translated by the authorised version.

What, therefore, Paul is prohibiting is not the exercise of authority by women as such but rather behaviour in leadership by these women that is manipulative, controlling and domineering. There are two reasons for this: the first is by implication that the Church is not to mirror the religious practices of the temple where the women rule supreme. The second is based on creation. Here, Paul says, Adam was formed first. The word for formed is *plasso*, from which we get the word plastic. It refers to how a person's knowledge and character is formed through learning. Adam was taught as he was formed first. He was given knowledge. However, Eve was not given any instruction and so was easily deceived. These women in Ephesus are similarly ignorant. They are easily deceived. Therefore, they must be taught.

3. So, contrary to this Gnosticism that these women are falsely teaching, child birth does not exclude one from salvation. Instead, says Paul, women will be saved if they truly believe and show the credibility of their faith through godly obedience.

What then are the implications of this passage for women and men in ministry today? We can conclude that today, as then, women and men are to publicly participate in worship.

On the basis of verse 12, some have sought to argue that whatever women may do in ministry they are never to teach men. Well, if that were so, it would mean that Paul is contradicting himself and would put him in conflict with the entire witness of scripture. And what would this make of Timothy whose entire spiritual education had been through the instruction of women, his mother and grandmother? And should women, on this basis, be excluded from becoming teachers or professors at a theological or Bible college? Would we be obliged to remove commentaries by women like Joyce Baldwin from our libraries? Would we remove hymns written by women like C. F. Alexander from our hymn books?

Should women be prevented from leading a home group Bible study where men are present? What about the hundreds of women missionaries we have sent abroad, should they have remained silent in the presence of men? Few would argue in this way. In practice, this verse is used only to prevent women from teaching men from a pulpit.

A more consistent handling of this passage is to see that in Ephesus heresy was being taught by women who were ignorant of the truth. Almost all women at that time were not taught. They were easily deceived. Their behaviour expressed their ignorance by being obsessed with their appearance in braiding their hair, buying fancy clothes and jewellery and in the domineering manner that they had learnt in the temple Artemis. They had taken to themselves or had assumed an authority which was unwarranted.

Women, say Paul, who do not know should not teach. So, 'let the women be taught'.

The application for today is that we are to ensure that men and women are well instructed in the scriptures. Our commitment to a balanced theological training for those in ministry has a solid base. It is the safeguard against heresy.

PASTORAL ISSUE FOUR

## *Electing Men and Women to Serve – The Jesus Way*

The story of the early Church is about women and men using their gifts freely to cause it to grow in maturity and in numerical strength. Both genders are in view when Paul writes:

> Let the message of Christ dwell among you richly as you teach and admonish one another with all wisdom through psalms, hymns, and songs from the Spirit.
>
> ✢ *Colossians 3:16*

Similarly in 1 Corinthians 12, the importance of discovering and using ones gifts to make the body grow is applicable to both men and women. We have already shown the long list of women and men serving in the Church.

All this was new. In the Old Covenant, women's ministries were restricted. Occasionally, as we have indicated, women were prophets and rulers but the central position of priesthood was restricted to men only.

In the New Covenant, because of Jesus, women and men together may be prophets and speak his word, they may be kings and rule, but now they have become priests and so may freely enter the holy place to meet

with God and to act on behalf of his people. This is radical and astounding.

> As you come to him, the living Stone –
> rejected by humans but chosen by God
> and precious to him – you also, like
> living stones, are being built into a
> spiritual house to be a holy priesthood,
> offering spiritual sacrifices acceptable to
> God through Jesus Christ.

> But you are a chosen people, a royal
> priesthood.

✝ *1 Peter 2: 4–5, 9*

The early Church was a period of life and freedom as empowered by the Holy Spirit, men and women exercised their ministries and the Church continued to expand. However, the community of faith needed accountability, order and governance. The Church had been founded on the apostles and prophets, which we have seen were both male and female but following the pattern of the synagogue 'elders'(bishops) and 'deacons' were *appointed* in the churches. We have come to call these offices.

Not surprisingly it is 'the pastoral letters' of Timothy and Titus, which deal with these issues. They were written much later than the gospels, the Acts of the Apostles and the other letters of the New Testament. John Calvin distinguished between temporary and permanent offices. The apostles, prophets and evangelists he believed were unique to the apostolic Church. He recognised four offices for today and they have become part of the Presbyterian tradition. They are pastors, teachers, ruling elders and deacons.

Certain people in the Church were recognised and 'set apart' in the community of faith for these leadership responsibilities. The New Testament material on the process

of appointment, commissioning or ordination is, to quote the late Professor David
Wright of New College Edinburgh, 'sus-
ceptible to different interpretations'. This is
the main reason we have different forms of
church government in the Christian Church.
In the Presbyterian or Reformed tradition,
there are different practices. In the PCI we
do not have 'deacons' as a distinct office but
it is subsumed under the church committee.
We do have deaconesses but not as an office.
Other Presbyterian churches have deacons
who are ordained, while others think
ordination is to a position of authority and
want only to commission them. In the
Church of Scotland, ruling elders are
'ordained' but not with laying on of hands
but through prayer by the minister. In the
PCI, ruling elders are ordained by the
presbytery with laying on of hands. In
Geneva and in Scotland during the sixteenth
century, the practice of 'laying on of hands'
of ministers was abandoned by the Church
for a period and ordination focused on the
'public call' of a congregation to a person for
a specific office.

However a person is to be appointed,
ordained or commissioned to the office of
leadership in the Church and whatever that

means, the Apostle Paul, nevertheless, sets out what is necessary to fulfill the office. He lists the requirements to be an elder (bishop) or a deacon in 1 Timothy 3:

> Here is a trustworthy saying: whoever aspires to be an overseer desires a noble task. Now the overseer is to be above reproach, faithful to his wife, temperate, self-controlled, respectable, hospitable, able to teach, not given to drunkenness, not violent but gentle, not quarrelsome, not a lover of money. He must manage his own family well and see that his children obey him, and he must do so in a manner worthy of full respect. (If anyone does not know how to manage his family, how can he take care of God's church?) He must not be a recent convert, or he may become conceited and fall under the same judgment as the devil. He must also have a good reputation with outsiders, so that he will not fall into disgrace and into the devil's trap.
>
> In the same way, deacons are to be worthy of respect, sincere, not indulging in much wine, and not pursuing dishonest gain. They must keep hold of the deep truths of the faith with a clear conscience. They must first be tested; and then if there is nothing against them, let them serve as deacons.

In the same way, the women are to be worthy of respect, not malicious talkers but temperate and trustworthy in everything.

A deacon must be faithful to his wife and must manage his children and his household well. Those who have served well gain an excellent standing and great assurance in their faith in Christ Jesus.

✣ *1 Timothy 3:1–12*

and in Titus:

Since an overseer manages God's household, he must be blameless – not overbearing, not quick-tempered, not given to drunkeness, not violent, not pursuing dishonest gain. Rather he must be hospitable, one who loves what is good, who is self-controlled, upright, holy and disciplined. He must hold firmly to the trustworthy message as it has been taught, so that he can encourage others by sound doctrine and refute those who oppose it.

✣ *Titus 1:7–9*

The language used here is masculine: 'He must manage his own family well and see that his children obey him', etc. Did Paul mean that only men could hold these positions, and that they must be married, have children (to show that they could manage their family), and be non-teetotal so as to prove they did not drink to excess? We think not. In those days all legal documents were male orientated. The Ten Commandments forbids husbands (men) from coveting their neighbour's wife, no one has concluded that this excludes wives (women) from coveting their neighbour's husbands! Similarly the divorce legislation was male focused (Deuteronomy 24:1–4) but Jesus had no hesitancy in applying it to women initiating divorce (Mark 10:12).

In fact 'the job descriptions' for the various offices in the Old Testament uses masculine language, even when they were offered to women. The classic example is that of a prophet where Numbers 12:6–8 says, 'When a prophet of the Lord is among you, I reveal myself to him in visions, I speak to him in dreams.' The language is about a man and yet specifically refers to Miriam (a woman).

What we have in these letters from Paul is not a crude 'checklist' for those who are to become leaders in the Church. Otherwise it would exclude single, childless, total abstainers. The emphasis of the Apostle is instead twofold:

1. The basic requirement for leadership as an elder or a deacon is character not

giftedness. What we are to look for is not what a person can do but rather who they are. We are to discern spiritual maturity in preference to personality, status or formal education. The only gift mentioned for an elder or bishop is the ability to teach.

2. The virtues we are to look for in a leader should model the new society which Jesus has created. A leader is to live consistently with who we are. It is at this point that we see again the setting out of the counter cultural nature of the Christian community. Paul deliberately chooses the qualities listed to show that Christian leadership is different from what was practised by the Greek and Roman world. In the Ecclesia, which was the centre of local government and the term Paul significantly uses to describe the Church, power was vested in a few wealthy and privileged people.

   ✢ Their lifestyle and moral choices bore no relationship to the responsibilities they carried.

   ✢ They were often polygamous with mistresses.

- ✝ Drunkenness and intemperance was the norm.
- ✝ They were indifferent to family life as long as their wives bore children who were then managed by a guardian.
- ✝ They used people to achieve their goals.
- ✝ The exercise of authority was in the Roman tradition with violence and naked power.
- ✝ They used their position for financial gain.
- ✝ They were normally despised by the general population.

Compare that to the character of an elder (or deacon) given by the Apostle.

- ✝ Trustworthy, with lives of integrity.
- ✝ Sexual faithfulness.
- ✝ Temperate and not a heavy drinker.
- ✝ Involved in the management of the family.
- ✝ People-focused, listening, developing respect and practising hospitality.

- ✤ Gentle and not a bully as a manager.
- ✤ Indifferent to money.
- ✤ Respected by those outside the Church.

This is the way all Christians should seek to live but it is especially so for those who would lead.

If the values and lifestyles of the new society are at variance with the world, Paul's standards means we also need to reflect on how Christian leadership puts us in conflict with the norms of leadership in western civilisation today. In Practice this would mean:

1. Christian leaders should not separate their private lives from their public responsibilities.

2. Whatever the sexual choices provided by society and its leaders, the Christian leader must remain sexually faithful in marriage.

3. The Christian leader will resist the pressure to place his business, company or church responsibilities above his responsibilities to his family.

4. The Christian leader will question business models which are so exclusively goal-orientated that people are mere pawns to be used to attain an objective. Similarly, they will question an obsession with modern technology which diminishes the importance and value of flesh-and-blood relationships.

As Paul had to compare Church leadership with what was assumed to be normal in his time, so, on the basis of his letters to Timothy and Titus, we ought to expect our elders (men and women) to have lifestyles and values which model the kingdom and place them in conflict with the patterns of this world.

I hope I have shown that the evidence from the scriptures in support of the Presbyterian Church in Ireland's position that women and men may share together as ruling and teaching elders is overwhelming.

The late Roger Nicole, Professor Emeritus at Reformed Theological Seminary, in Orlando expressed it like this:

> I believe that most, if not all, the restrictions on women in society have no basis in scripture; and that those maintained in the church are based on an inadequate interpretation of a few restrictive passages

which put them in contradiction with the
manifest special concern and love of God
for women articulated from Genesis to
Revelation. I do believe that in the
'eschaton' all the redeemed will endorse
biblical equality, since all of them will
together constitute the bride of Christ.

## Practical Steps

There are many practical steps that can be taken to developing a church where women and men are equal and complement each other in leadership. On the basis of what our church believes, let me set out four ways which might be helpful in putting this into practice.

*Create a church community where women and men are encouraged to exercise their gifts with enthusiasm and freedom.*
No one believes that only men have been gifted by God for ministry. Latent within our churches are resources which need to be released. Here are some examples:

- ⚜ Practical and pastoral caring, especially the ability to listen.
- ⚜ The practice of hospitality.
- ⚜ The welcome of strangers without being either gushing or indifferent.

- Gifts of praise in the use of musical instruments, the human voice and the leading of worship.
- The ability to use modern technology effectively.
- The public reading of scripture with understanding.
- The gift of evangelism and the training of others within the congregation.
- The leading of home groups.
- The ability to teach children, youth and adults the scriptures.

- ✢ A gift of writing to be used in articles for church newsletters or local newspapers.
- ✢ Gifts to develop the spirituality of the congregation.
- ✢ A ministry of public prayer.
- ✢ A willingness to help!
- ✢ Catering.
- ✢ The development of the arts and the aesthetic in the life of the Church.
- ✢ Abilities in matters financial.
- ✢ A commitment to develop the mission of the Church in Ireland and around the world.
- ✢ Encouragers.
- ✢ People who will build a bridge between the Church and the social needs of the community.
- ✢ Men and women who enjoy fixing things!

The list is endless. It is in the exercise of such ministries that women and men will develop a sense of equality as they complement each other as co-workers with Christ.

*Ensure that women are invited to deliberate at session meetings, especially if they are exercising leadership in some aspect of the Church's ministry.*

Many of our Kirk sessions are exclusively male. This may be because of tradition or theological conviction. Whatever one's view about authority and headship in marriage, it would be a daring husband who never consulted with his wife. It is in discussion and consensus that decisions are made. Similarly, it does seem odd that women are not at least consulted at elders' meetings when matters relevant to their giftedness and ministry are being discussed. In the Presbyterian Church, the SPUD initiative, where young people, although not voting members, are invited to deliberate and even propose resolutions at the general assembly illustrates this. It is a model which could be developed at a local level, where women and men can be invited to sit and deliberate. There is precedent. Redeemer Presbyterian in New York, although restricting the eldership to men, has all the leaders of each department of ministry at the session meeting, regardless of gender.

*Be more proactive in encouraging women to become elders or ministers.*

In churches with a tradition of only electing men to the ruling eldership it requires enormous courage for a woman to be willing to serve. It is necessary, as part of the process of election, to read to the congregation from the Code (par. 31) that 'women shall be

eligible for election on the same conditions as men'. But I am suggesting that something more is needed, namely that the congregation know why, on the basis of scripture, women and men may be elected. This is one of the reasons for writing this book. The congregation may then become proactive in seeking out men or women who have the maturity and godliness to act as elders. Women would not then be so reticent.

It is fascinating that to become a ruling elder, the objective 'call' precedes the subjective. Namely, the congregation chooses and those so elected are invited to respond either positively or negatively. In the 'call' to the ministry we expect a person to have a subjective sense of call which is then confirmed or otherwise by the local and then the wider Church. Some women, who have had a growing sense of call, because of the negativity towards women pursuing the ministry, have offered to serve abroad through a mission agency or the Board of Mission Overseas. They then proceed to do overseas what was frowned on in Ireland. This has no sense to it, except as Tony

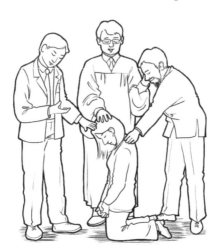

Campolo says, 'We do not believe in women preachers unless they are preaching to blacks!' We should encourage women who we discern have the potential to become ministers of the word and sacraments. Invite them to lead the worship, conduct prayers, address the children or even preach. The congregational response will help in the confirmation process. In this sense we would be more proactive.

*Recognise that the differences of the place of women and men in ministry within the PCI are so small that it ought never to be a cause of division.*

Consider the areas where everyone is in agreement.

- ✝ Women and men equally share the image of God.
- ✝ One is no way inferior to the other.
- ✝ They are joint heirs of the salvation secured by Christ.
- ✝ They both have received the Holy Spirit.
- ✝ They have both received the gifts of God to build up the body of Christ.

- ✝ Women and men are free to instruct and teach each other from the scriptures.

- ✝ We honour both women and men as theologians, Bible teachers, hymn writers and spiritual directors.

- ✝ We recognise women and men who have been prophets and leaders of worship.

The areas of disagreement are small. In reality any disagreement on this subject is in a very narrow area. Some, on the basis of their reading of 1 Timothy 2:12, although believing that women and men should be free to preach and pastor, are not persuaded that a woman should be permitted to exercise a certain type of authority in the Church. Susan Foh, a New Testament scholar, who supports this view says that in all of scripture 'this [passage] is the only adequate reason for not ordaining women'. This has led some of our ministers and elders 'for conscience's sake' to seek to be excused from services of ordination and installation of women, which they are permitted to do.

If we believe from scripture that men and women can preach, teach, pastor, disciple, serve and witness, what then is this narrow area of authority which would be restricted to men only?

Those who hold this view seem to argue that there are three such areas:

1. To admit or dismiss people from the church.
2. To do 'quality control' of members doctrine.
3. To act as 'tie breakers' in matters of disagreement.

It does seem odd that a women CEO is not competent to do this, or that a highly trained female biblical scholar is not able to assess 'sound doctrine', or that someone with a speciality in conciliation cannot be the 'tie breaker', simply because of their gender. Nevertheless these arguments reveal a quite different focus of eldership than we have in the PCI. As elders, we major in policy decisions and in the pastoral care of the congregation. This is why some large congregations have between forty and sixty elders so that districts or 'little flocks' will be adequately cared for. We are also responsible for receiving and removing church members as well as overseeing soundness of doctrine but, in practice, all of this is the work of a Kirk session, presbytery or the general assembly and not of ministers. This is when elders work together. This came home to me when I was in Bangor. I was part of a committee of the general assembly under the late Alan Flavelle. Our task was to assess the Shepherding movement, as it was called. Its influence on many young people in Hamilton Road Church was considerable. At the heart of their contention was that you submitted to the rule of Christ by submitting to the rule of your shepherd or elder. It began to fall apart when we were able to show them from scripture that on every occasion, without exception we are encouraged to submit or defer to 'the elders' in the plural. We are never asked to submit to an elder as an individual. In the Presbyterian Church, elders function together, at general assembly, presbytery and in Kirk session. The minister, who is not a member of the local church but the presbytery, is simply the moderator of the session. So, in Presbyterian polity no man has authority over a woman and no woman can have authority over a man. Men and women together, therefore, have authority over men and women. The ordination of a woman to the ruling or teaching eldership does not give her authority over any one man or woman. The issue, therefore, of a woman having authority over a man does not apply.

For decades, whatever one's views, men and women in the PCI have functioned courteously and graciously with each other in the courts of the church. Ruling and teaching elders have never seen the position of our denomination on the ordination of women as being a cause of division and, perhaps even more significantly, few have seen this as such an issue of conscience as to prevent them from seeking office in a church whose policy and practice is to ordain women and men to the ruling and teaching eldership.

# Final Thoughts

Lesslie Newbigin the English missionary statesman said:

> The gospel does not become public truth for a society by being propagated as a theory or a world view and certainly not as a religion. It can become public truth only insofar as it is embodied in a society (the church) which is both 'abiding in Christ' and engaged in the life of the world.

This is how we are to be. When Harvie Conn (of Westminster Seminary in Philadelphia) was at the first residential general assembly in Coleraine, he emphasised that the Church was 'the show house', the model which people viewed before they made a decision. We are meant to show what it will be like when the new day comes, when a new heaven and a new earth has been established. We are the children of the day which is to come. Jesus Christ through his life, death and resurrection has already established what will be. What was lost through our moral defiance of God with all its consequences will be undone.

The equality of men and women and the full display of their masculinity and femininity as they complement each other in ruling over the new creation will be unveiled. At that point we will perfectly express what it means to be 'in the image of God'. We will be truly free to love God and to love each other as we serve as leaders together.

As we live in anticipation of what has been promised, we, as Christ's Church are to be the sign of the new creation. In our leadership we are to express this as Jesus showed us and the early Church lived it. It will create for us pastoral and cultural issues in its application which may be different from that addressed by the Apostle Paul.

In Ireland today we are torn between two extremes. On the one hand, there is pressure to maintain a hierarchical, male-ordered society, where roles are stereotyped for macho-men and sensitive women. In this women feel excluded from the real decision-making. On the other, under the influence of radical feminism, an equality agenda has so minimised the differences between the genders that men are struggling with their identity and the expression of their masculinity.

In the application of the Jesus way, we will embrace neither. Equality does not mean equivalence and difference does not mean domination.

In the Church men and women should be free to lead but never to the detriment of their manhood or womanhood. Instead, they will rule together in collegiality because men need women and women need men. This is how we truly express the image of God and say to the world – a new day is coming and this is how it's going to be.

## *Resources*

There is a spectrum of opinion on this subject by those who have a high view of scripture.

The traditional view of the Church for hundreds of years was that women may not share authority with men in leadership. Women were excluded from specific ministries in the Church. Only a cursory reading of Church history demonstrates that this was because the prevailing Greek and Roman view was that women were inferior to men by nature. The Church came to embrace this notion. Augustine, Tertullian, Chrysostom, Jerome and others argue in this way. By the time of the medieval Church this was normative thinking, as one finds in the writings of Thomas Aquinas. The reformers were a product of the Medieval Latin Church. Calvin and Luther both contended that by nature women are not created 'to govern'. They were patriarchal in their thinking. Christian patriarchy seeks to maintain this traditional view: it is held e.g. by R. C. Sproul, Jr and Douglas Wilson.

Two new views emerged in the twentieth century from those who were seeking to discern from the Bible the relationship between men and women in leadership. They take their names from the primary emphasis of their conclusions.

*Complementarianism* 'affirms that men and women are equal in the image of God, but maintain complementary differences in role and function. In the home, men lovingly are to lead their wives and family as women intelligently are to submit to the leadership of their husbands. In the church, while men and women share equally in the blessings of salvation, some governing and teaching roles are restricted to men.'

*(www.cbmw.org)*

*Egalitarianism* holds that 'all believers – without regard to gender, ethnicity or class – must exercise their God-given gifts with equal authority and equal responsibility in church, home and world'.

*(www.cbeinternational.org)*

Within these two views there are shades of opinion. You will find hard complementarians like John MacArthur and increasingly John Piper who would exclude women from all leadership roles in the Church and home to insure that they are under the authority of men. There are also soft complementarians like Tim Keller, whose church allows women to lead in almost every sphere of pastoral and teaching ministry and in marriage 'practises' mutual submission. In the home he believes the man ought to be the 'tie breaker' when consensus is not possible. Men, he argues, should alone be responsible for the oversight of a congregation.

Similarly there are hard egalitarians that are happy to be described as evangelical feminists. Rachel Held Evans would be one of these. In her writings, equality and equivalence is difficult to distinguish and gender difference is minimised. Soft egalitarians like John Ortberg would encourage equality for both genders in the service of Christ. Nevertheless, the gender differences would be recognised and celebrated in the home and the Church by him. In practice, he encourages leadership in specific areas of ministry according to maturity, competence and knowledge rather than role categories.

You may find the following helpful in that they articulate in more detail the reasons for the stance of the Presbyterian Church in Ireland on this issue:

✢ Almost anything written or spoken by Kenneth E. Bailey, the New Testament scholar and Presbyterian missionary.

Specifically:

*Jesus Through Middle Eastern Eyes: Cultural Studies in the Gospels* (SPCK Publishing, 2008).

*Paul Through Mediterranean Eyes: Cultural Studies in 1 Corinthians* (SPCK Publishing, 2011).

*Women in the New Testament: A Middle Eastern Cultural View* (http://www.theologymatters.com/JanFeb001.PDF).

✢ Gaebelein Hull, Gretchen, *Equal to Serve: Women and Men Working Together Revealing the Gospel* (Baker Book House, 1991).

✣ Bilezikian, Gilbert, *Beyond Sex Roles: What the Bible Says about a Woman's Place in Church and Family* (Baker Academic, 2006).

✣ Johnson, Alan F., ed., *How I Changed My Mind about Women in Leadership: Compelling Stories from Prominent Evangelicals* (Zondervan, 2010).

✣ Pierce, Ronald W., and Groothuis, Rebecca (gen. eds), Fee, Gordon D (contributing ed.), *Discovering Biblical Equality: Complementarity Without Hierarchy* (IVP Academic, 2005).

✣ Ortberg, John, *What the Bible says about Men and Women* (Menlo Park Presbyterian Church) (http://www.willowcreek.org.uk/resource.php?r=276).

✣ McKnight, Scot, *The Blue Parakeet: Rethinking How You Read the Bible* (Zondervan, 2008).

✝ McKnight, Scot, *Junia Is Not Alone: Breaking Our Silence About Women in the Bible and the Church Today* (Patheos Press (kindle), 2011).

✝ Guinness, Michelle, *Woman: The Full Story: A Dynamic Celebration of Freedoms* (Zondervan, 2003).

✝ Tidball, Derek & Dianne, *The Message of Women: Creation, Grace and Gender* (IVP, 2012).